VANISHING
WILDERNESS

VANISHING
WILDERNESS

AMERICA'S LAST WILD PLACES

J.A. KRAULIS

ARROWOOD
PRESS

Page 1: Dogwood tree in bloom, Pacific coastal rain forest.

Page 2: Cottonwoods grow beneath great sandstone cliffs in a widening of Buckskin Gulch, Utah.

Published in 1989 by

Arrowood Press
A division of LDAP, Inc.
166 Fifth Avenue
New York, NY 10010

Published by arrangement with Key Porter Books Ltd.

Library of Congress Catalog Card Number: 89-84131

Aerial photography on pages 16, 17, 30, 34, 44, 45, 46, 47, 48, 50, 52-53, 56, 57, 60, 61, 62, 81, 97, 104, 109, 139, and 140 produced in collaboration with pilot Bo Curtis.

ISBN: 0-88486-028-0

Printed in Italy

CONTENTS

INTRODUCTION 9

THE MOUNTAINS 13

LAKES AND RIVERS .. 41

THE FORESTS 65

THE DESERTS 93

THE COASTS 119

To active environmentalists everywhere, with admiration and gratitude

Left: A subalpine meadow with false hellebore and lupine, Minarets Wilderness, Sierra Nevada, California.

Below: A small waterfall in the deep woods of southeastern Mount Rainier National Park, Washington.

INTRODUCTION

Our water is contaminated, our air is corrosive. Our soil is being mined of its nutrients or flushed into the sea. Too little ozone threatens us with cancer. Too much carbon dioxide is creating a greenhouse effect that could flood our coasts while turning our interior plains to dust bowls. Millions of species from beetles to blue whales are in imminent danger of extinction. The rain forests are being systematically wiped out. The food chains of the oceans are in danger of collapse. Overpopulation, poverty and starvation plague scores of nations, and the global economy is hamstrung by the manufacture of deadly drugs and weapons.

In the face of such dire environmental problems, it may seem futile and even unimportant to worry about wilderness and its preservation. But environmental issues are all interrelated, and protecting the last remnants of primeval earth is, in some ways, the most significant of them all.

In the wilderness lies the source of all that we know and all that we have. The first tools, the first building materials, the first domesticated plants and animals came straight from the wilderness. Everything we make and grow, everything we consume or utilize has its ultimate origin in nature, even if the lineage is long and indirect. We have only begun to understand the depth of that source, wherein still lie the possibilities of endless discoveries. In rare, endangered plants may exist the genetic combinations that hold the secrets to new medicines and new foods. Perhaps new navigation technologies will come from solving the mystery of how certain creatures are able to migrate long distances without losing their way. Whales and dolphins, among other endangered species, may give us profound insights into the evolution of communication and language. We still haven't found adequate answers to many basic questions, such as why do we sleep. In the wilderness lie the answers to questions we have not yet even thought to ask.

Although wilderness has great scientific and practical worth, its most compelling value is spiritual. The experience of wilderness, like that of art and athletic endeavor, can be profoundly valuable and yet immeasurable by any economic yardstick. Other environmental issues are primarily concerned with survival, but that of wilderness also concerns our soul.

We live in two often intermingled but radically opposed worlds, the man-

Tundra flowers growing on sand underlaid by ice in Auyuittuq National Park, "the land that never melts," Baffin Island.

made and the natural. Wilderness gives us the opportunity to experience our deepest roots, to understand things from a very essential, different perspective. The absence of wilderness, with civilization confined only to the world of its own making, is unthinkable. It would represent the ultimate loss of freedom.

It is ironic that "democracy" is invoked by some as an argument against setting aside many wilderness areas. Those who want ever greener pastures for their cars, their all-terrain vehicles, snowmobiles and powerboats argue that opening up more wilderness means making it accessible to a greater number. But machines can destroy delicate environments and, at the very least, turn it into something that is no longer wilderness.

To fully experience wilderness requires much the same conditions as it takes to experience a symphony. One needs time and an undisrupted setting. Driving up to some mountain lake, spending a few minutes taking in the scene, and then driving off again is a bit like walking into a concert hall, listening to the orchestra for a few enjoyable moments, and then leaving. One could readily appreciate that the symphony was beautiful, but one could not claim to have experienced it.

To understand wilderness and its value, one needs to understand time. We value things because of their age and because of how long it took to make them. A gothic cathedral, several hundred years old, is considered priceless; no amount of a developer's money could ever budge it. The North American wilderness is a heritage much longer in the making. Virgin west-coast forests have taken a thousand years or more to reach their climax stage. But we talk of "harvesting" the timber as if it were merely some patch of oversized corn; a few minutes is all it takes to fell a tree twice as old as the European occupation of this continent. Many of our most beautiful valleys and canyons are millions of years old. The dams that drown them are only considered economically viable if they pay for themselves within a few decades. The time it took for a species to evolve is the longest of all, as mind-numbing to contemplate as the distance to remote galaxies. All life is the product of billions of years of change on the earth. Wolves, grizzly bears, sea lions and other wildlife are cut down by the gun of a rancher or a fisherman. These won't come again, even after another four and a half billion years.

Once, there was nothing but wilderness in North America. It took us little more than a few decades to shoot, chop, burn, dig and pave our way from one coast to the other. That is an incredibly short time, much less than the age of Europe's best cathedrals. It should give pause to the engineers, executives and politicians who feel that it is of little consequence to chip away a bit at the little wilderness we have left.

Understandably, the need to protect wilderness cannot be fully understood by those who have not experienced it. In an ideal world, everyone should. Wilderness is like music. It confronts us with the most profound and wonderful of mysteries. It is fundamentally impossible to describe or explain why it moves the spirit so deeply. Its elimination from human experience would leave a tremendous void. Wilderness reminds us of what a wonderful world this is and what a wonderful world it still can be.

THE MOUNTAINS

It seems impossible. High up in the slowly swirling sky where one should see only more cloud, there appears a whiteness too bright to be a cloud. As the clouds move, the whiteness remains stationary until more of it is revealed, as snow and ice ascending and disappearing towards the still concealed summit. Emerging out of the thick Alaskan weather and rising above it is the tremendous mass of Denali, "The Great One." Nowhere else, not even in the Himalayas, does a mountain rise farther above its timberline and snow line.

Beyond the base of Denali (also known as Mount McKinley) and the other giants of the Alaska Range, the colorful tundra stretches unblemished in all directions, a browsing and foraging ground for diverse and abundant wildlife. One does not have to travel far or wait very long to see several cariboo, a moose, a herd of Dall sheep, a grizzly with cubs, pair of wolves, a fox, an eagle or perhaps all of these. The only road into the park is eighty miles of dirt. Backpackers will find no footpaths to guide them, no bridges to help them across wide glacial rivers.

Here, in Denali National Park, is wilderness the way it should be— unmarked, unbounded, fecund and majestic. But there is not enough of it. Quotas and other restrictions are placed on vehicles and hikers allowed into the park. Wilderness is a fragile and scarce thing; it must be rationed, even in the wide, open heart of Alaska.

It is rationed in many other regions as well, in national parks such as Jasper, Banff, Yoho, North Cascades, Mount Rainier, Glacier, Yellowstone, Grand Teton, Rocky Mountain, Yosemite, Kings Canyon, Sequoia, not to mention other designated wilderness areas. In order to preserve wildlife, fragile vegetation or simply the wilderness experience, it has been necessary to impose limits on the number of people allowed into a wilderness, how long they may stay and where they may camp.

Gone are the days when people could ride into such places, their horses chewing up decades of alpine flower growth in a single grazing; when campers could tamp down any virgin plot with their tents and make a fire from the scarce wood at timberline. This is the age of the gas stove, the lightweight boot and biodegradable soap.

It is becoming the age of the roped-off wilderness. As trails turn to

---

An alpine rock garden below the granite cliffs of Eastpost Spire in the Bugaboos, British Columbia.

trenches and meadows to mud, major measures have been taken in some of the more accessible places in our mountain parks. The footpath through the profusely flowered slopes above Paradise in Mount Rainier National Park has been paved, and it is prohibited to stray from it. Similarly, a boardwalk protects the vibrant alpine meadows at Logan Pass in Glacier National Park. Conservation is achieved by keeping people out of nature, in queues on their own ground.

The mountains are being loved to death for the straightforward reason that they are beautiful. Full of bracing air, clean waters and fresh flora amidst plunging and soaring vistas, they launch the spirit. Few would be roused to argue John Ruskin's statement that "Mountains are the beginning and the end of all natural scenery."

All that rock-solid scenery is mostly the result of the plasticity of two materials, one of plutonic and the other of celestial origin. In a manner not yet fully known, the flow of hot, solid but pliable rock deep below the surface drives the movements of the great tectonic plates that make up the earth's crust, movements which (as has been realized for only a few decades) create mountains. North America rides on one of the plates, which has been moving rapidly westward (at about the speed at which fingernails grow) for the last sixty million years, overriding other plates under the Pacific, and heaving up at one time or another all of the varied ranges of the western Cordillera.

It is an extremely complex but fascinating geological story, one involving the birth of oceans and the splitting and merging of continents; one with surprising details, for example, the likelihood that the rocks of which Denali is made were part of some distant Pacific island millions of years ago.

As immense as these forces are, the scenery owes most of its shape to plastic movement of another kind, to the creep of glaciers formed by layers of snow. Erosion has carried away much more of the mountains than what now remains.

Solid, plastic and heavy, glaciers erode the landscape in a different way than rivers do. Vertical cliffs, matterhorn peaks, U-shaped valleys with thousand-foot waterfalls leaping off the sides exist only because they were sculpted by glaciers.

The cliffs of Yosemite were shaped and polished by ice that filled the California valley at one time or another over the last two million years, although in today's mild climate, there isn't a glacier in sight. Comparable granite verticality exists in cirques and valleys elsewhere, such as at the headwaters of Arrigetch Creek in the Brooks Range of Alaska, in the Cirque of the Unclimbables in the Yukon Territory's Logan Mountains, and in several places on Baffin Island, where some of the cliffs—dead vertical or even overhanging—are four thousand feet high.

Throughout the mountains, glaciers have left behind thousands of alpine basins dotted with innumerable lakes, cascading creeks, weather-sculpted trees, flowering meadows and rock gardens. The mountains' beauty is a combination of these intimate, accessible foregrounds and the awesome backdrops. It is a young land, and it makes one feel young. Not surprisingly, one sometimes encounters people in their eighties with canes in the timberline regions. The modest challenge of walking against the hill to reach some little unspoiled paradise is intoxicating to everyone who undertakes it.

Away from the dammed, logged or paved valleys, the alpine slopes and basins continue to offer, if not true wilderness by a purist's definition, at least an excellent illusion of it. But that vanishes with the tentacles of asphalt trails that grow out of too-near parking lots. Proponents of drive-through wilderness argue for more easy access, as if having enough highways to keep a tourist driving for several lifetimes isn't already enough. In order that we may see more and more of less and less, the road advocates advance the specious argument that the mountains shouldn't be for just a "hardy few." What they will achieve instead is just more rationing of the truly beautiful places.

Divorced from earth, the high, white reaches of Denali represent perhaps the last wilderness. There is a stark and sculptured beauty among ice fields like these. There is vast space and often a profound silence. Here there is nothing to cut down, nothing to cultivate, no reason or way to build settlements or roads. It is a place where only the skilled and the strong can go. There will always be a wilderness experience for the hardy few, but perhaps not for the rest of us.

Left: An aerial view of the unglaciated Richardson Mountains, just north of the Arctic Circle in the Yukon.

Above: Seen from the air, a rain shower falls on the Dawson Range south of Dawson City, Yukon.

Banner Peak in the Minarets Wilderness, Sierra Nevada,
California. Deep snow still covers the high regions in May.

Becalmed for several days in early October, a lake reflects The Totem in St. Mary's Alpine Park, British Columbia.

In the stillness of dawn, Baron Lake reflects Monte Verita and
Warbonnet Peak in the Sawtooth Range, Idaho.

High over the Bugaboo region of the Purcell Mountains, British Columbia, clouds catch the light of the setting sun.

Above: Above the timberline in autumn on Algonquin Peak, the second highest summit in the Adirondacks, New York.

Right: Wallface Mountain in the Adirondacks in midwinter.

Willow herb blossoms on the edge of a tundra pool in the Weasel
Valley, Auyuittuq National Park, Baffin Island.

A glacier and its moraine in the blue shade of a cold, late winter afternoon in Eremite Valley, Jasper National Park, Alberta.

Lake Oesa and Mount Ringrose, Yoho National Park, British Columbia.

Moonrise and Mount Olympus, Olympic National Park, Washington.

Above: Seen from the plains, Chief Mountain is an unmistakable landmark of Glacier National Park, Montana.

Right: The 2,200-foot vertical face of Half Dome in afternoon light, Yosemite National Park, California.

Above: Garibaldi Park, British Columbia in the winter. Mount Baker, Washington is on the center far horizon.

Right: The Saint Elias Mountains of Yukon and Alaska contain some of the most spectacular glacier landscapes on earth.

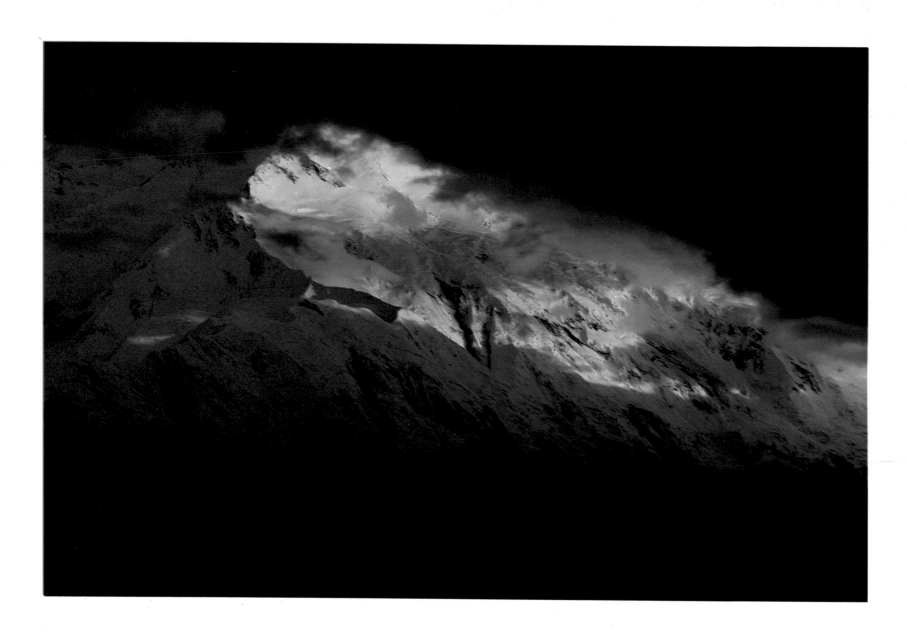

Parting clouds reveal Denali on an Alaskan evening. The summit of the immense mountain is three-and-a-half miles higher than its base.

Through an opening in the clouds, the sun spotlights aspens in autumn below the Maroon Bells, Colorado Rockies.

Above: Confluence of the South and North Kaskawulsh glaciers, Kluane National Park, Yukon Territory.

Right: Unmelted snowdrifts in August on Black Tusk, looking towards the Tantulus Range, Coast Mountains, British Columbia.

Left: Willow herb, arnica and Indian paintbrush growing amidst rocks above timberline.

Above: The Angel Glacier and the moraine and meltwater lake of the Cavell Glacier, Mount Edith Cavell, Jasper National Park, Alberta.

The Consolation Lakes and a small portion of the tremendous view
of the Rockies from the summit of Mount Temple, Banff National
Park, Alberta.

After sunset, the moon rises over Mount Niles in Yoho National Park, British Columbia.

LAKES AND RIVERS

It is inherent in miracles that they seem to come from nowhere. The microscopic beginnings of a human life are too small to be seen by the unaided eye. The universe itself, according to prevailing theory, was born as a tiny point, exploding out of the void.

So it is with clouds, which appear literally out of thin air. All that we know of nature is, in large measure, the product of those clouds. Terrestrial life depends utterly on all the fresh water that has been distilled in clouds. The land itself owes its shape to rain and snow, splitting ice, grinding glacier and rushing water. Lakes and rivers are another phase of the miracle— they are clouds come to earth.

When their emergence is not delayed in lake or glacier, rivers are the more immediate metamorphosis of clouds. They can be born in minutes in the desert as the gathered contents of a thunderstorm. Rivers are magic. They cast spells on us. They undergo endless transformations, coasting or cascading through every kind of geography, animating each in myriad ways. Many grow out of the confluence of brooks in high alpine basins. Trees follow some of them out of the forest, clinging to their banks as they take Pied Piper jaunts across grassland or desert. A few rivers reach the sea in great deltas, in a fan of channels, ponds and lakes.

Rivers invite metaphors. A river represents a journey, a gathering, life, time and more. We think of rivers as young, or as old, or as both. Many rivers have been running for a very long time; those that are not found in glaciated terrain are older than all the landscape that surrounds them. The Colorado River, for example, has been in existence longer than the Grand Canyon, which it created.

Of course, in technical geographic terms, a river is young where it runs steep, straight and boisterous; old where it loops lazily across flats. Among the most interesting are rejuvenated rivers where such meanders have become incised deep into the land. On the Colorado Plateau, in particular, there are numerous wild, serpentine canyons. The canyons of the Green and San Juan rivers are among the largest and offer unusual opportunities for river running.

Life and rivers are interallied. Life swims in rivers, barren areas are nourished to life by rivers, and rivers are alive in the real sense that they

Lake O'Hara and Mary Lake and the Great Divide, Yoho National Park, British Columbia.

are never still and always changing. They are the lifeblood of a land. Rivers deposit soil and nutrients on their floodplains and deltas. There they also create wetlands, important habitat for a wide variety of wildlife from muskrats to moose, and which are indeed vital for the great flocks of migratory waterfowl.

"A wanderer is man from his birth. / He was born in a ship / On the breast of the river of Time," wrote Matthew Arnold. To float downriver through a wild valley is to journey through the wilderness in perhaps the most appropriate and profound way possible, carried along on the return side of one of nature's grandest cycles. With time, one becomes attuned to the idea that the river is life and life is the river.

All that a river is and all that it offers dies when a dam is built. Gone are the winking riffles, the roaring waterfalls, the countless animated little landscapes of swept sand or rounded stone along the banks. The upstream side becomes a vast drowning—death for the flora as well as their mothering soil, and eviction for the fauna. Downstream from the dam, destruction usually follows: the flow to habitats is disrupted, the dam-filtered river without its sediment load quickly erodes away the sandbars and beaches it deposited over centuries.

In the lower forty-eight states, rivers that run free are scarce; rivers that run wild and free are very rare. Even a designated wilderness waterway like the Allagash in Maine has three dams on it, while permits to go down many of the best wild rivers are available only through lottery or long waiting lists.

Compared to rivers, lakes are transient features of the landscape, but they exist in great numbers. From tiny tarns like Lake Tear-of-the-Clouds, the source of the Hudson River, to the freshwater seas of the Great Lakes, there are several million lakes in North America. The vast majority are glacial in origin, and a few of these are an integral part of some of our most wonderful landscapes. The creamy aquamarines and turquoises of the lakes of the Canadian Rockies come from the light scattering of suspended fine silt washed down from surrounding glaciers. In the Sawtooth Range of Idaho, lakes in the granite bowls left by glaciers now gone are so numerous that it is often possible to find campsites between two lakes that are only a few dozen yards apart, and sometimes perhaps even connected by a small waterfall.

But by far most of the lakes on the continent are found in a roughly eight-hundred-mile-wide swath around Hudson Bay, coinciding with the location of the granitic billion-year-old Canadian Shield and that of the continental ice sheets which weighed down the land a hundred centuries ago. The retreat of the ice left behind uncountable excavations and depressions in the rock, which filled into a vast maze of waterways so bewildering that even from the air it is often difficult to tell where one lake ends and another begins, whether the land below is island or peninsula.

Nowhere else on earth is there a comparable profusion of fresh water. Among the endless chains of lakes are dozens so large that the opposite shore is out of sight beyond the horizon. At the same time, there is a superabundance of intimate landscapes in millions of islands. There are 14,632 islands on Lake of the Woods alone, while the Thirty Thousand Islands of Georgian Bay are three times more numerous than their name suggests.

From Maine through the Adirondacks in New York to Minnesota and northward all the way to the Arctic are opportunities for the longest and remotest of wilderness excursions. These recall a time when lakes and rivers were the main—in many areas the only—means of movement across the land, a time when once virtually the whole continent was wilderness, little more than a few generations ago. (Could we really have consumed so much of it in so little time?) The canoe provided the original wilderness experience and remains its most ready symbol.

A canoe inverted on the stone shore of a pine-scented island, a flickering campfire beside the silhouette of a tent, the long, lonely call of a loon or a wolf coming from some ambiguous direction far across the water on a still night: that's quintessential solitude. One might be tempted to add roasting fish to the scene, but not these days. In some places the fish come from waters that may have been seasoned with a dash of mercury, a pinch of dioxin, or perhaps a few buckets of PCBs. Most of the time, though, there are no fish.

On a long canoe trip, there is no better time for contemplation than when rain falls with a soothing drumming on the tent roof. Perhaps one thinks of the clouds, and beyond them to the ocean, the source of the clouds, the grandmother of rivers. Long ago, so it is believed, even the oceans themselves were born out of clouds, condensed out of a roiling atmosphere of volcanic gases. It can be disturbing to think too much about the rain itself. Acid rain is the reason that the lakes are sterile and that there are no fish. And the acid rain is ruining more than just the fishing. It is eating away at forests, farms, even our health. The clouds are not what they used to be.

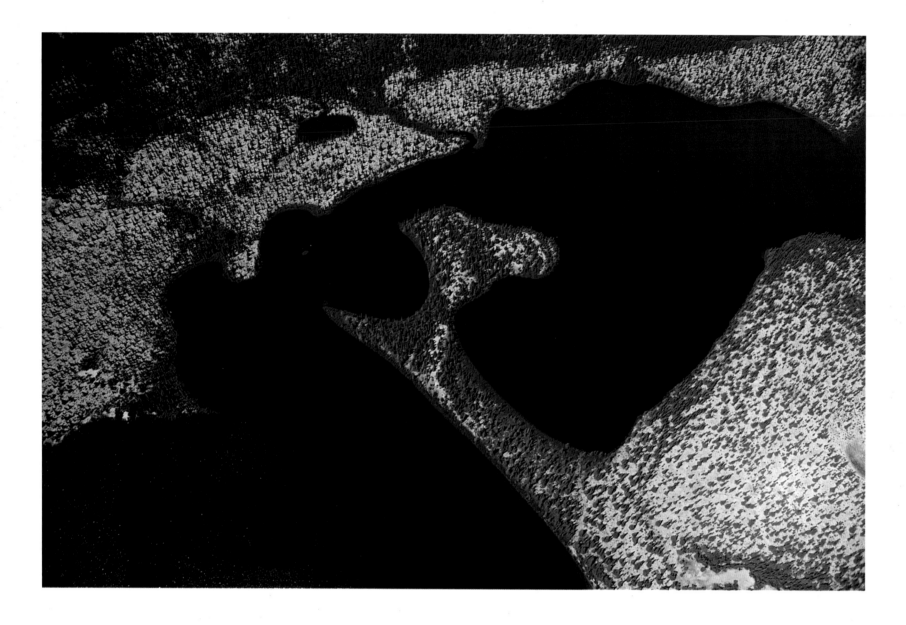

Above: An aerial view of the Canadian Shield near the Quebec–Labrador border, a region of uncounted lakes and open boreal woodland.

Right: A mixing of glacial waters seen from the air. The Slims River, dense with silt, enters turquoise Kluane Lake, largest in the Yukon.

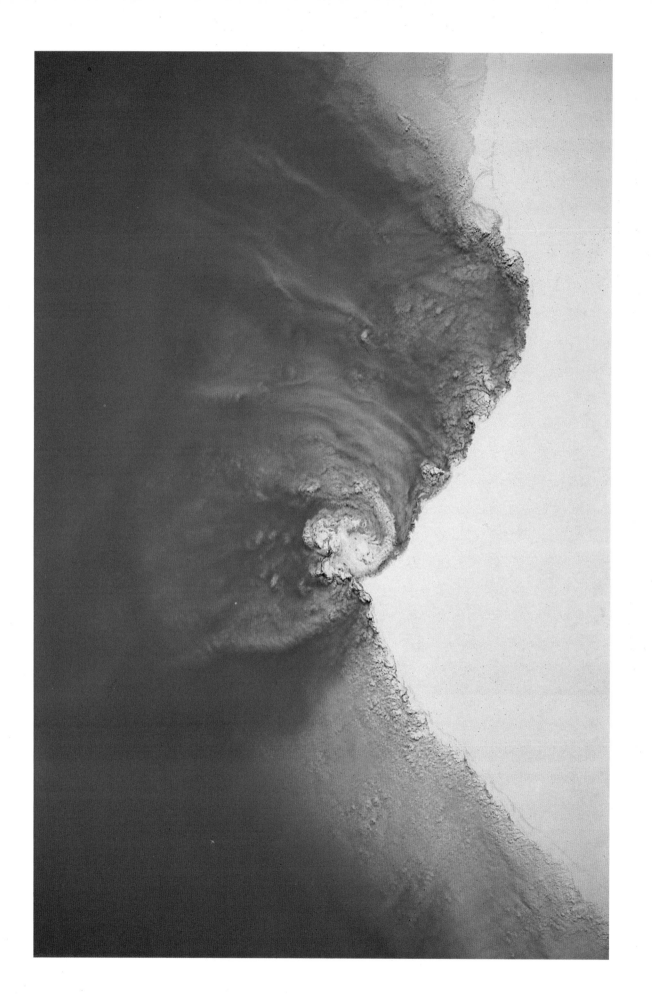

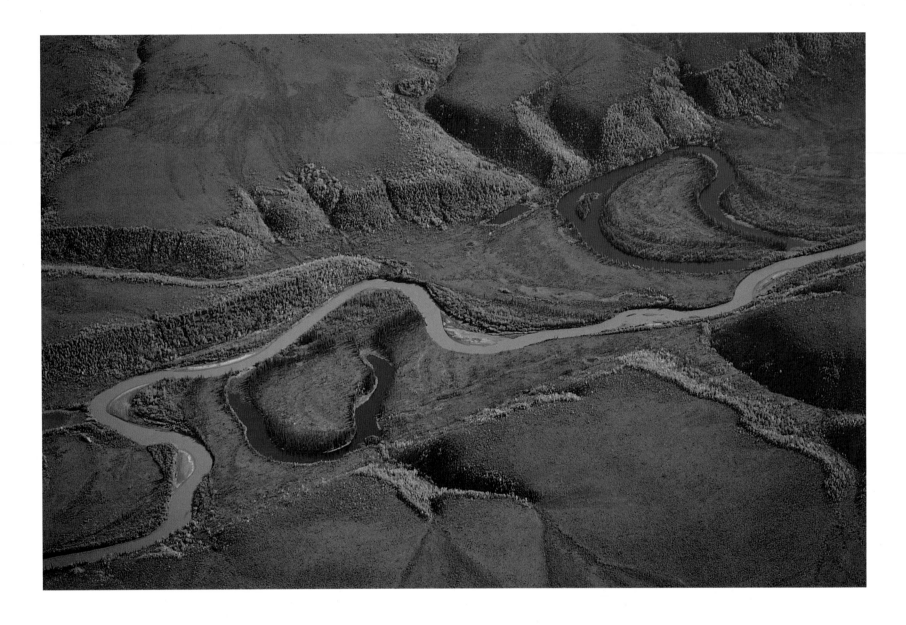

Above: An aerial view of a river north of the Ogilvie Mountains, Yukon Territory. Clearer, settled water distinguishes the oxbow lakes from the parent stream.

Right: Uplift of the Colorado Plateau created the incised meanders of The Goosenecks, San Juan River, Utah.

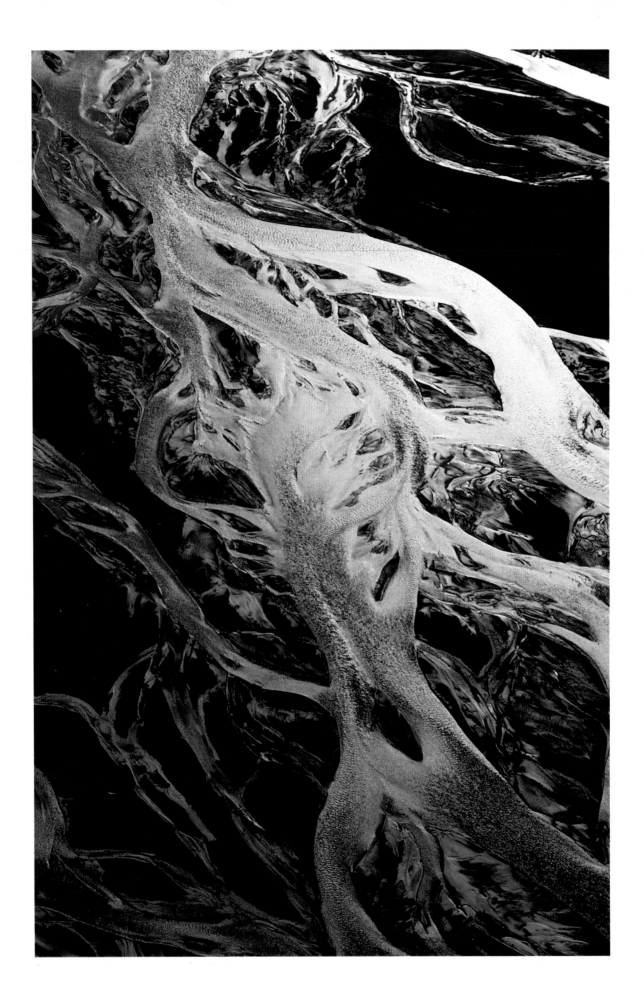

Left: The Kaskawulsh River is one of numerous braided streams carrying the meltwater of huge valley glaciers in the Saint Elias Mountains, Yukon Territory.

Above: A channel of the North Saskatchewan River winds across the flats of a glacial valley in northern Banff National Park, Alberta.

Above: Churchill Falls, Labrador, Newfoundland, is the second most powerful cataract after Niagara in North America.

Right: Spahats Creek Falls, British Columbia, was created by differential erosion where the stream encountered softer, volcanic rock.

Above: Reeds reflected along the mirror-quiet shore of a lake at dusk.

Left: A remote lake (probably unnamed) in a treeless basin of the Ogilvie Mountains, Yukon Territory.

Left: Explosive Donjek Falls in Kluane National Park, Yukon Territory, carries the heavily silted meltwater of numerous large glaciers.

Above: Ouiatchouane Falls, Val Jalbert Park, Quebec is one of the innumerable cascades of the Canadian Shield.

Above: An aerial view of a small group of granitic islands off the north shore of Lake Superior.

Right: Georgian Bay at sunset with a few of the Thirty Thousand Islands, the world's largest freshwater archipelago.

Left: The North Saskatchewan River, Alberta, flowing through an aspen forest in the fall.

Above: Rising in Maine, the Shogmoc River flows towards its confluence with the Saint John River, New Brunswick.

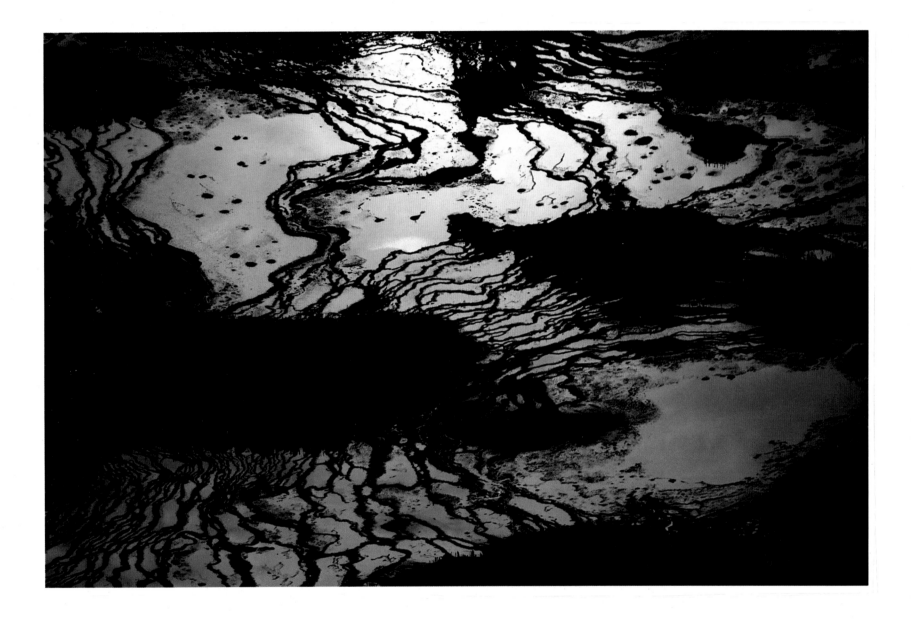

Left: A small fraction of the several thousand lakes and channels which constitute the great Mackenzie River Delta, Northwest Territories.

Above: An aerial view of string bog, a common feature of low-lying northern landscapes.

A creek cuts through the unglaciated Kluane Ranges, Yukon.

The intense blue waters of Crater Lake, Oregon.

THE FORESTS

There are wild places which, through sheer immensity alone, can overwhelm all of a visitor's expectations. Such is the trailless trek across the tundra under the ever-soaring, ever-distant white ramparts of the Alaska Range, or the seemingly endless stepped descent into the multicolored depths of the Grand Canyon.

But of the different kinds of grandeur in nature, perhaps the most wondrous of all is one where the scenery is the product of biology rather than of geology. In western North America, still preserved in a few shrinking pockets, are grand canyons of wood, forests containing the greatest trees on earth.

Among these are the renowned redwoods that grow along the mist-nurtured coast of northern California. Redwood forests contain more living matter per square unit of area than any other environment, primarily because the redwoods themselves are the tallest living things on earth. A large specimen laid low would stretch the length of a football field, including the end zones. Sitka spruce and western hemlock, huge trees on their own, also grow among the redwoods.

In winter, a redwood forest is dark and moody, dripping with continual rain. Profuse white trillium and pink rhododendron blossoms brighten its floor in the spring. During the fogs of summer, the summits of the trees disappear out of sight, literally into the clouds. Lush in any season, it is a forest of perfect, plumb trunks rising several hundred feet without a noticeable taper, silvery or rusty columns a dozen feet in diameter, holding up vast arenas of cool, shimmering green.

A famous public servant from California once offered the callous opinion that, "If you've seen one redwood, you've seen them all." But if you have seen full-grown redwoods, allowed yourself to marvel at their size and thousand-year age, to be moved by their elegant form and the ever-remarkable fact that they are alive, you could not contemplate the cutting down of even one such tree without sadness.

And while one redwood is a marvel, a redwood forest is much more than that, something far greater than the sum of its enormous parts; it is a sanctuary, a place that elicits ineffable emotions. In a few parks, it is still possible to have the remarkable and profoundly calming experience of

Falls and flowers in the lush forest of Mount Rainier National Park, Washington.

walking through continuous old-growth redwoods for an entire day. Such a trip represents an opportunity to retreat in time in two senses. On the one hand, it is an entry into an undisturbed primeval forest that has been in the making for several thousand years, much longer than any civilization. On the other hand, to walk down corridors of trees that seem too big to be real is like a return to childhood, to a time when everything in the world was so much bigger and seemingly reassuringly indestructible.

But for our children, the forests of the future (if indeed any are left), will be much smaller. As you read this, the remaining virgin stands of redwoods continue to shrink. Most are in private ownership, waiting to feed one of the world's most lucrative timber industries. Within many groves of old-growth redwoods, the machine noises of logging intrude from the distance. Frequently one hears and feels the reverberations of a powerful, ground-shaking boom, and one may pause to wonder why dynamite is being used in a modern logging operation, until one realizes that the sounds are not explosions, but the crashes of giant redwoods falling to earth.

Other great western species of trees are disappearing just as rapidly. Within the narrow strip of abundant rain and mild winters along the Pacific coast, the Douglas fir, Sitka spruce and western red cedar are each capable of growing to sizes comparable with the redwoods. In fact, measurements at the turn of the century suggest that Douglas firs grew to heights greater than the present-day 367-foot record for a redwood. One that was felled at the beginning of this century near Vancouver was recorded to be 415 feet long.

Today, the tallest known Douglas firs are a three-hundred-foot-high group on a small island in the middle of the gravelly Nimpkish River on Vancouver Island. At their rate of growth, it is possible that within a human lifetime, some of them may actually reach higher than the tallest redwood. But just as possibly, as part of a current timber license without any protected status, they may be cut down.

The same fate may befall a forest in the Carmanah Valley on Vancouver Island, which includes the tallest tree in Canada, a Sitka spruce that reaches 312 feet. Under license to be cut are also the oldest living trees in Canada. On Meares Island along the British Columbia coast is a magnificent forest of red cedars, many of which are more than a thousand years old and nearly twenty feet in diameter. So far, their logging has been prevented mostly by legal maneuvers concerning native land claims, rather than by much political appreciation for the idea that, in an exceptional case like this, the value of the woods is vastly greater than the value of the wood.

The most immense trees of all are not redwoods nor any of the other coastal species. Growing in a few dozen separate groves on the western slopes of the Sierra Nevada in California, the giant sequoias are the most massive living things on earth, and likely the most massive that ever lived. While the redwoods grow taller and many have trunks as wide as an average room, some giant sequoias are as wide as a good-size house, approaching thirty feet in diameter at the base. With rich red bark (as much as two feet thick), metallic green foliage and fine proportions, the sequoia is as beautiful as it is huge.

If ever there was a natural phenomenon to inspire universal awe, and for which the need of preservation was clearly evident, that phenomenon would be the rare giant sequoia grove. Yet shortly after these trees were first discovered by white men in the middle of the last century, the best stands were destroyed. Trees thirty centuries old were cut down primarily for shingles, fence posts and grape stakes. Evidence remains to indicate that some of these were larger than any still in existence. One was felled after several days of laborious effort for the vulgar novelty of having its stump as a platform on which thirty couples could dance at a time. Due to considerable conservation efforts at the turn of the century, old giant sequoias, now located mostly in national parks, continue to exist. Unfortunately, so does the kind of mind-set that nearly resulted in their eradication.

Eastern North America once had very big trees, too. Magnificent forests of white pine ranged from Nova Scotia south through the Carolinas. These are gone now, virtually all stands of the largest, old-growth specimens logged by the end of the last century. But the forests of the Appalachians and the southern part of the Canadian Shield are, at a certain time, the most spectacular on earth. Each fall, maples, birches, beech, ashes and other hardwoods combine to make the eastern woodlands into one of the most vividly colored of all landscapes.

This too is now under siege, not by logging, but by other industries hundreds of miles removed. Acid rain is eating away at the trees, the most brilliant, the maples, being the most seriously affected. Dieback is conspicuous on the tops of many, and it is hard these days to find an unblemished scarlet leaf, one not pitted or spotted.

We rightly decry the razing of tropical rain forests. Meanwhile, in North America, we have the world's largest trees in the west, the most colorful in the east. At an accelerating rate, we are toppling the last of the former and bleaching the life out of the latter. The wastelands we see elsewhere are appearing in our own backyards.

Left: Lichen on the bark of a sugar pine, Kings Canyon National Park, California.

Above: Trunks of giant sequoia, sugar pine (center) and white fir (covered with lichen) in Sequoia National Park, California.

Above: Cedars, junipers and pines on a granite apron near Tenaya Lake, Yosemite National Park, California.

Right: Snag of a whitebark pine in the Sawtooth Range, Idaho, after an early September snowfall.

Western larches retain their autumn gold into early November;
frost covers the trees and bushes at the moist valley bottom.

Their trunks conspicuous early in May, white birches prevail on a sunny hillside on the Canadian Shield.

Left: Autumn colors on the slopes of Giant Mountain in the Adirondacks, New York.

Above: Fall colors in the Muskokas, Ontario. The forests on these two pages are among many affected by acid rain.

Above: Giant sequoias are the most massive trees on earth and among the rarest. This is Lost Grove, Sequoia National Park, California.

Right: One of many huge trunks along the Miners Ridge Trail in Prairie Creek Redwoods State Park, California.

Alpine larch in autumn. Found only at the timberline, this
deciduous conifer often grows into weather-beaten forms with much
character.

Sugar maple saplings in autumn. Stands of this striking species, responsible for so much of the color of eastern forests, are being decimated by acid rain.

Above: Dogwoods blossom along the Stamp River on Vancouver Island in early spring.

Right: An aerial view of deciduous forest near the Maine–New Brunswick border in early summer.

Above: Autumn frost and a young eastern white pine.

Left: Lodgepole pines and aspens in the Rockies in late September.

Left: A fire-scarred giant sequoia, white fir boughs and the lichen-covered trunk of a white fir in Sequoia National Park, California.

Above: The alpine larch adds splendor to the few western mountain ranges where it grows.

A monarch butterfly on autumn migration settles on a goldenrod in
the woods on Pelee Island in Lake Erie.

Maple, aspen, beech, willow and other fallen autumn leaves float in the pool of a small brook.

Above: Distinguished by deep red bark, a manzanita grows beside Cascade Creek in Yosemite National Park, California.

Right: Hung with moss, ferns and its own very large leaves, a bigleaf maple is part of the lushness of the coastal rain forest.

Left: A red maple, with its splendid autumn foliage, near the Atlantic Coast.

Above: The most widely distributed of North American trees, aspens color large areas in the fall.

THE DESERTS

The desert is an enigma. It is a land inevitably defined by what it lacks. The word may evoke images of big cactus or big sand dunes, but in most deserts neither is predominant nor even existent. Defining it by what it is not—waterless, treeless, uninhabited, uncultivated, barren—admits the fact that the desert defies easy summary.

Perhaps nowhere is this more the case than in the deserts of the American Southwest. Here there are snow-white gypsum dunes, jagged black lava flows, towers and arches of orange sandstone, hills painted in mineral hues of purple, turquoise and amber, wide chasms through bands of rock displaying a rainbow's range of color, and narrow gorges with many different colors created by the physics of indirect light. How can one succinctly describe a land that contains a Grand Canyon, a Death Valley, a Petrified Forest, a Monument Valley, a Zion Canyon, a Bryce Canyon, the region of Arches and that of Canyonlands, to name only a few of the best known? None of these places even remotely resembles any of the others, although somehow, ineffably, all seem to belong distinctly to the desert.

The amazing variety of formations which occur in the desert are found, for the most part, only in the desert. From buttes, badlands and bajadas to salt flats, slot canyons and sheer-sided sandstone slabs, all sorts of weird and wonderful landscapes are but the direct result of naked stone and its infrequent encounters with thunderstorms. The desert is the pure, unadorned face of the earth, not masked by forest nor veiled by dazzling waters.

The desert is also a place of apparent contradictions. It is a dry land, generally hot, but it owes most of its appearance to the freeze-thaw cycle and to flood. Contrary to a common misconception, wind accounts for very little of the shape of the desert, except for sand dunes. The muddy and often violent runoff after a rain has great, if intermittent, scouring power. Unglaciated and without the restraining effects of vegetation, the "waterless" desert exhibits the effects of fluvial erosion more clearly and more abundantly than any other kind of landscape.

Life is the source of another desert contradiction. Generally thought of as inimical to life, the deserts are home to a surprising number of species. Two or three thousand different kinds of plants thrive in the Sonoran Desert

---

Cactus forest, Saguaro National Monument, Arizona.

alone, and some places contain a greater variety of flora than many forests. Some of the most extravagant flower blooms also occur in the desert, an explosion of color immediately following rain at certain critical times of the year. And within the desert are the oldest living things on earth. High in the dry mountains of Nevada and eastern California grow the bristlecone pines. The oldest ever discovered had survived for more than 5,000 years before it was cut down by a scientist for the sole purpose of determining its age. Parts of some living creosote bushes are believed to be even older, perhaps as much as 10,000 years.

Of the various regions of the Southwest desert lands, the most remarkable must surely be the Colorado Plateau, an elevated area contained mostly within southern Utah and northern Arizona that is drained by the Colorado River. There are so many towers, spires, arches, hoodoos and other upright formations on the Plateau that one writer appropriately named it "Standing-Up Country." But even more spectacular features are below the surface of the plateau. This is a land full of canyons, preeminent, of course, being the Grand Canyon.

Cut straight down in sandstone by gritty floodwaters gathered from a distance, the narrowest, known as slot canyons, are often several hundred feet deep while only a few feet wide. In exploring such subterranean corridors there is the risk of a flash flood, the possibility that the contents of a remote thunderstorm might come rushing down the canyon at a point from which there is no escape. High above the canyon floor, mud-caked logs jammed between the sheer walls occasionally attest to the depth of these flash floods.

A variant of the slot canyon is the incised-meander canyon, where a looping watercourse has eroded outwards as well as downwards at each bend, carving immense vaults in the sandstone. The interior of such a canyon is like a series of alternating, linked half-bowls turned on their sides. One walks between curving, overhanging walls which culminate in roofs of stone that in some instances span a width of several hundred feet.

As intimidating as these desert canyons may seem, they are at the same time staggeringly beautiful. In few other places on earth will one find a more sculptured landscape, or one more magically illuminated. The stark, direct light of the sun seldom reaches the canyons' depths where in the occasional wide alcove an island of green cottonwoods may grow. Instead, the canyons are suffused with the glow of light bounced and rebounced off the walls, with golds, oranges and subtle shades of purple where these blend with the blue from the skylight overhead.

The canyon names tell an agonizing story of a desert destroyed and a desert threatened. There are the fanciful and fabricated names, such as Jadi Canyon, Dragon Canyon, Tao Canyon. And there are the lost names, Music Temple, Cathedral in the Desert, Glen Canyon. The fanciful names sanctioned in print on postcards and in magazine articles, have been invented by people who feel strongly that it is in the best interests of the wilderness that the locations of certain canyons, which are hard to find, remain secret. They have a strong case. A slot canyon would be filled up with people as rapidly as it fills with floodwater, destroying its solitude and mystery and making it about as appealing as a subway in rush hour. And in numerous canyons, morons have defaced delicate walls with graffiti and bullet holes or vandalized centuries-old ruins and petroglyphs.

The lost names argue another case. Glen Canyon is the name of a national recreation area. The canyon itself no longer exists; it and over a hundred tributary canyons were flooded with the completion of a dam across the Colorado River. Places like Cathedral in the Desert and Music Temple, once among the finest desert landscapes in the world, were lost forever, as were innumerable places never even documented. Bitter debate over Glen Canyon Dam continues three decades after its construction. Of limited value for water control and electricity, it is defended with reference to the boating opportunities created by its reservoir, Lake Powell, and to the fact that it is now easy to get to some places which were once only accessible to the "hardy few." The latter argument makes about as much sense as cutting down a stand of redwoods in order to get a better view of a few Sitka spruce. As for the recreational opportunities, a great cathedral has been destroyed to make way for an amusement park. Even those who defend the dam would pause if given the opportunity to go back in time to see what the reservoir drowned.

Other dams have been proposed that would eliminate more canyons. Along with its extraordinary tributary, Buckskin Gulch, Paria Canyon is one place which some wish was a better kept secret. But at one time, there were plans to dam this tremendously deep and narrow canyon and its little stream solely for the purpose of reducing sediments which rains would wash into a reservoir behind a dam proposed for the Grand Canyon itself. Such destructive plans still exist in some filing cabinet, stymied only by voices for the wilderness.

The most poignant name in the desert is the one that never was: Escalante National Park. First proposed in the thirties, it would have preserved Glen Canyon and all its awesome and magical side canyons. But too few people were aware of the wonders that this land contained. The title of a book on the subject sums it up best: Glen Canyon was "The Place No One Knew."

Hoodoos from Inspiration Point, Bryce Canyon National Park, Utah.

Badlands from the air near Blanding, Utah.

Left: Nolina are part of the fascinating flora near the Santa Maria Canyon, Arizona.

Above: Blossoms and an approaching thunderstorm in October, Ernies Country, Canyonlands National Park, Utah.

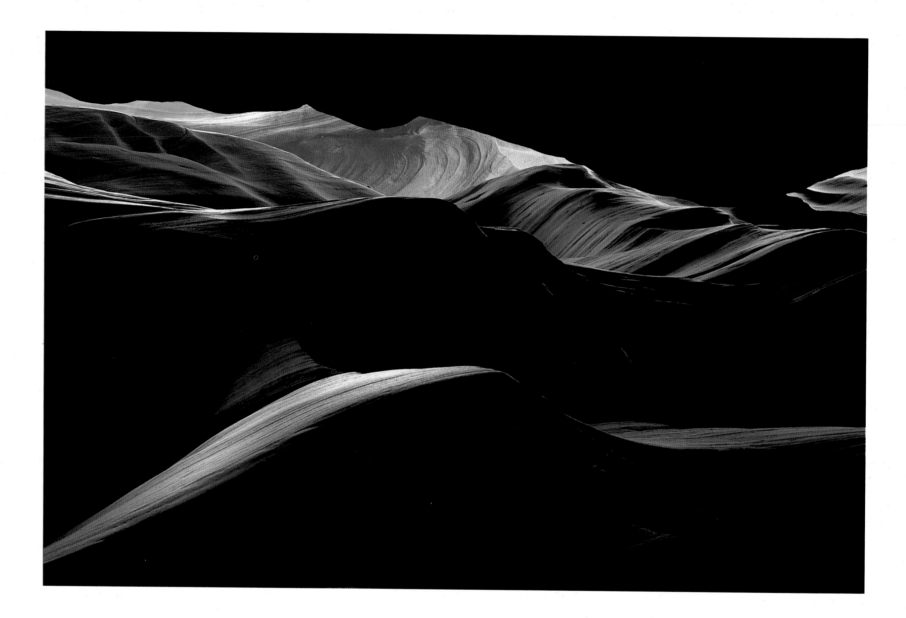

Inside a narrow slot canyon. The golds and oranges come from sunlight bouncing off the sandstone walls; the blue is reflected skylight.

This slot canyon near Page, Arizona, is littered with garbage and scarred with graffiti, some of which can be found within the picture.

Above: At Great Sand Dunes National Monument, the dunes rise seven hundred feet above their surroundings.

Right: Beetle tracks cross one of the dunes near Stovepipe Wells, Death Valley National Monument, California.

Above: Monument Valley, Arizona, from the air.

Right: Cloud shadows across the Painted Desert, Petrified Forest National Park, Arizona.

Left: Wind-fashioned dunes and flood-carved mountains, Death Valley National Monument, California.

Above: Bristlecone pine in the arid, thin air at twelve thousand feet in the White Mountains, California.

Above: Desert paintbrush growing amidst chert, Arches National Park, Utah.

Right: Deva, Brahma and Zoroaster (nearest) Temple from the air at sunset, Grand Canyon, Arizona.

Left: Reflection in a side canyon of Forbidding Canyon, Rainbow Plateau, Utah.

Above: Beautifully carved sandstone walls and arching spaces are among the charms of desert slot canyons.

The mineral-stained hillside of Artist's Palette is one of numerous
improbably-colored landscapes found in Death Valley National
Monument, California.

Only very occasionally does a bush with deep-spreading roots break the expanse of the world's largest gypsum dunes at White Sands National Monument, New Mexico.

Left: Very high walls keep most of Paria Canyon, Utah, in the shade.

Above: Davis Gulch, Utah. Many sandstone canyons on the Colorado Plateau have huge overhanging walls cut by sweeping flash floods.

Storm clouds behind The Fins, Canyonlands National Park, Utah.
This remote region of Canyonlands National Park is rarely visited.

Dusk at White Sands, New Mexico. Plants such as yucca,
squawbush, rabbitbrush and saltbush sometimes find a toehold
between the dunes.

THE COASTS

One vast blue ends and another begins on the remote and long horizon where the sky meets the sea. Regular as breath, waves rolled by thousand-mile winds rush into shore and expire on their last crest. As the earth turns, the rising and falling tides trace the rise and set of a distant moon.

Allied with great distances and grand rhythms, the rim where continent meets ocean holds our most fertile and dynamic wilderness. No other wilderness is home to as rich a diversity of life dwelling in two different worlds, the marine and the terrestrial. The coasts are never silent and never still. Perhaps no other can offer the experience of wilderness within so confined an area.

A canoeist needs an area expansive enough to contain a long river, a hiker, a long trail. But just to sit on a hidden beach or some wave-smashed point may give a comparable feeling of an unspoiled corner of the world. The vista moves on its own, the surf drowns passing noise, the offshore winds bring only brisk air. The ocean is the great escape, for the mind as well as for the sea mammals that bask on the rocks. Occasionally the coast is but a few hundred yards from civilization. One can describe a highway-hugged coastline such as that in Oregon as wild, although pavement is no more than a mile away, and often even closer.

Most of the North American coast is, in fact, uninhabited and utterly isolated from any road, accessible only by aircraft or boat: the Arctic Islands, Hudson Bay, the fjords of Labrador and British Columbia, Alaska (which alone has a longer coastline than that of the rest of the United States combined) as well as a few jungle and desert shores of Mexico. But for the lower forty-eight states and the more populated regions of Canada, the coast is prime real estate, a coveted thin strip where any sense of solitude is created by the sea and not by distance. Virtually nowhere is it possible and practical to wander along this more accessible coast for more than a day without encountering habitation.

There are two exceptions, two sections of coast (within an easy drive of major cities) where one can beach walk and backpack at the same time, camping next to breaking waves a day's walk from the nearest trailhead. Both are on the Pacific coast, separated from each other by only a few dozen miles. One is traversed by the West Coast Trail in the southern

Desert rocks smoothed by ocean waves, Baja California.

portion of Pacific Rim National Park on Vancouver Island, the other is the coastal section of Olympic National Park in Washington.

Here one can be thoroughly immersed in wilderness while wandering in step with the caprices of surf and tides, breathing the washed, salty air, sleeping to the alternating snore and sigh of the restless ocean. On the one hand, there are pools with sea stars, sea anemones, mussels and other intertidal life; on the other, a forest so dense that it would take the better part of a day to bull through just a few hundred yards of it, were it not for the primitive trails.

The trails, which need constant clearing, are needed to get around numerous impassable rocky headlands, but in general one stays on or as close to shore as possible. Much of the Olympic coast consists of wide, long sandy beaches overlooking large numbers of spectacular sea stacks. The West Coast Trail section is somewhat remoter and rougher, the shore in many places being a rocky bench below short cliffs which is passable only at low tide, if at all, and which presents the potentially fatal risk of being trapped by an incoming tide. All depends on the weather. During winter storms, waves can knock a person down a hundred feet from shore. At any time, the high tide may sweep farther up the beach than expected, instantly inundating one's campsite.

These two wild coastal walks are unique. But while both are in designated national parks, neither is protected and, at present, neither can be protected from ruin. They are threatened by a very particular and different kind of destruction: that caused by accident. Pacific Rim and the coastal section of Olympic National Park are on opposite sides of the entrance to the Strait of Juan de Fuca, one of North America's busiest shipping channels, leading to Seattle, Vancouver and other ports. The risk of an oil or chemical spill in the region is ever present.

On December 22, 1988 a tug collided with its own barge in stormy seas off Grays Harbor to the south of Olympic National Park. A quarter of a million gallons of oil were spilled and carried northward by currents, narrowly missing the Olympic beaches, but fouling seventy miles, or most of the length of Pacific Rim National Park. What limited cleanup was possible involved hundreds of people and took a month. Retrieved from the beaches were some eleven thousand oil-soaked dead birds representing over thirty species, and representing no doubt only a portion of those actually affected. The full and long-term impact of the spill remains unknown; damage could have occurred to populations of gray whales, sea lions, sea otters, nesting eagles and intertidal life.

This was only a small spill. The two national parks involved are near large population centres with ready resources of machinery and people. A much wilder and correspondingly richer coast lies further northward in British Columbia and Alaska. Tragically, a few months later, on March 24, 1989, the largest oil spill in North American history occurred when a tanker out of Valdez grounded, spilling fifty times as much oil into Prince William Sound as was lost in the Washington spill. The news reports were grim. The world's largest colony of sea otters faces extinction and the full consequences to wildlife won't be known for months or years. They will be devastating. And it's only a matter of time until the next spill.

To a great extent, the health and abundance of wildlife is the best measure of wilderness. If the ultimate wilderness is that which is the most alive, then some of the best candidates for that wilderness would be found along the northeastern coast of the continent, in isolated islands and capes that serve as seabird sanctuaries. Among the most versatile of all creatures, seabirds spend most of their lives on the open ocean, out of sight of land. Each spring they assemble in great colonies at a few dozen precipitous, surf-beaten sites. Puffin, petrel, murre, kittiwake and gannets nest in the tens of thousands; the first two in burrows, the next two on every little ledge and projection that can be found on a sea cliff face, while the gannets crowd sea stacks or other prominences so densely that from a distance, the rocks appear white-capped.

The air, the ground, the waters all around are full of life. Profoundly moving, such places can make a person weep. One weeps at the beauty of it all. But one weeps too for all that is now gone. Once, the buffalo, antelope and elk roamed the prairies in the tens of millions, egg-laying sea turtles hauled out and covered southern beaches, huge flocks of passenger pigeons darkened the sky, wolves and whales were abundant. Sights which past generations witnessed, we will never see. What is it that our children and grandchildren will never see?

One weeps for the seabirds themselves. The largest of their number, the great auk, became extinct in the last century, clubbed to death for food. The present-day colonies themselves may soon cease to exist. Oil wells are to be drilled near some of the most important colonies, such as the Witless Bay Sanctuaries in Newfoundland. Worse, research indicates that the birds are starving; the stocks of capelin, a small fish on which they and indeed much of the marine food chain depend, are being overfished. The day may come when, besides the surf, all that one will hear will be the sound of silence.

Above: Moon and sea stacks after sunset, Samuel H. Boardman State Park, Oregon.

Right: Moon and wave-eroded rocks on a beach near the southern tip of Baja California.

Low tide reveals starfish and barnacles along a beach at the north
end of the coastal section of Olympic National Park, Washington.

Enderts Beach, Redwood National Park. Northern California has a spectacular coast as well as the world's tallest trees.

Cape Flattery, Washington, northwesternmost tip of the lower forty-eight states.

Yuccas and the Pacific near Big Sur, California.

Above: Waves during a winter storm, Cape Breton Highlands National Park, Nova Scotia.

Right: A surge channel near Wya Point, Pacific Rim National Park, British Columbia.

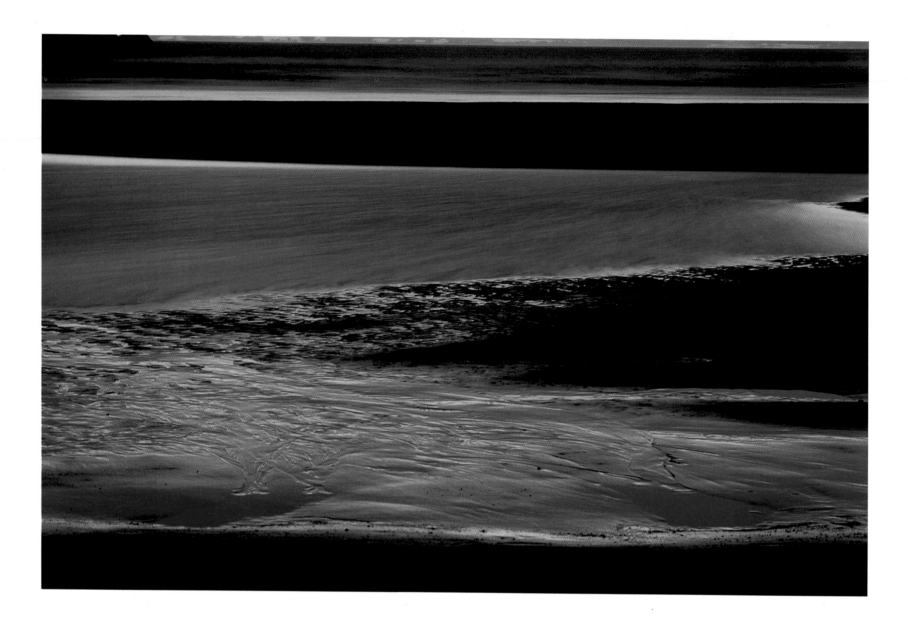

At low tide on a beach in southern Oregon, the rich colors of deep
dusk suffuse wet sand, a pool and the ocean.

Sunset silhouettes ice floes stranded by low tide at the entrance to Pangnirtung Fjord on Baffin Island.

Melting in a beached ice floe creates a window for this view
towards Cumberland Sound from Pangnirtung, Baffin Island.

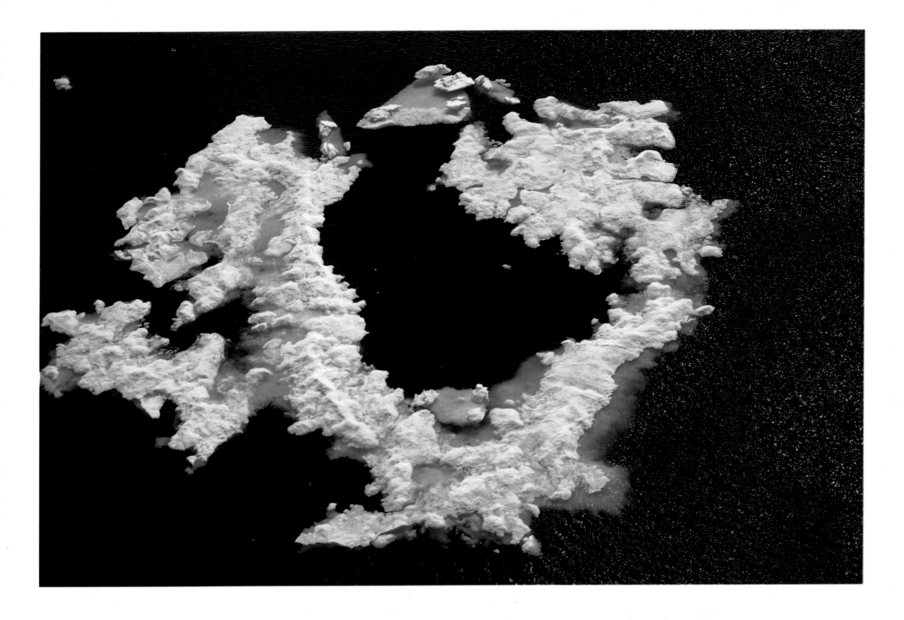

An aerial view of an ice floe in arctic waters. Melt on the surface of such frozen sea ice is drinkable fresh water.

Above: Île Bonaventure, Quebec is home to one of a few spectacular gannet colonies found on northern Atlantic coasts.

Right: A beach of smoothly rounded stones eroded from basalt columns on Brier Island, Nova Scotia.

Left: Covered with gannets, Bird Rock contains but a small portion of the nesting seabirds at Cape St. Mary's, Newfoundland.

Above: A long exposure of surf at sunset near Pigeon Point, California.

Spectacular sea cliffs and wide sandy beaches mark Cabo San Lucas, the extreme tip of the Baja Peninsula.

An aerial view of waves from the Gulf of St. Lawrence breaking on a beach in Prince Edward Island National Park.

Left: A sandbar in the Strait of Georgia, British Columbia, seen from the air.

Above: Calved from giant glaciers in Greenland, large icebergs drift southwards on the Labrador Current for three years before melting away.

Left: Lichen-covered shore rocks and tide-uncovered sea rocks at the entrance to the Bay of Fundy.

Above: Sea stars at low tide along a beach in Olympic National Park, Washington.

Sea gulls on the Pacific coast near Netarts, Oregon.